Children's Activity Book & Journal
My Trip to Iceland

TravelJournalBooks

Copyright © 2015 TravelJournalBooks

All rights reserved.

ISBN-13: 978-1511438704
ISBN-10: 1511438703

CONTENTS

Hi, I hope you enjoy this book. It is jam packed with cool stuff for you to do from crosswords, word searches, drawing, coloring and quizzes. It has loads of fun things for you to do in Iceland

What's Inside	Page
For your Parents	4
Before you go to Iceland	5-14
Cool Places to visit in Iceland	6-7
Research Iceland	9-11
Postcard & Packing List	12-14
Activities to do on the way to Iceland	15-33
Puzzles, cool facts, drawing and coloring	
Iceland Trip Diary	35-63
14 day trip diary to record cool things from your trip	
Activities for the Trip Home	65-81
Quiz, drawings and Memory Journal	
Resources for Mom & Dad	83-86
Puzzle Answers & Solutions	87-101

Have FUN in ICELAND

FOR YOUR PARENTS

We hope you enjoy your trip and thank you for buying our book, keep it safe as it is a great keepsake of your child's early years.

If you like this book, please leave us a review or provide feedback.

We have books for a number of holiday destinations at:

www.TravelJournalBooks.com

Bonus:
We have provided a bonus for you on page 83. We hope it helps.

This is my Journal

My Name: _____

Age: _____

Parent's name: _____

Tel: _____

Address: _____

_____

Important Information

Cool Places in Iceland for Kids

Blue Lagoon	✓
Reykjavik Zoo	
Perlan Building Viewing Deck	
Gullfoss (Golden Falls) Waterfall	
Lake Myvatn	
Breiðafjörður	
The Cathedral at Holar	
Strandarkirkja	
Skógar Museum	
The Arctic Fox Centre	
National Museum of Iceland	
The Saga Museum	

Aurora Reykjavik	
Akranes Museum Centre	
Reykjavik Botanic Garden	
Sudavik	
Hof Farmhouse	
Arnarstapi	
The Saga Museum	
The Cinema Old Harbour Village	
The Golden Circle	
Northern Lights	

Do your own research to find out what other places you would like to visit

Best Websites to Research Further

Do some more research on the internet and add other cool places you find:

www.TravelJournalBooks.com/Iceland   We keep this fully updated with the best places
www.wikipedia.org/wiki/Iceland
www.planiceland.com
www.visiticeland.com
www.iceland.is
www.visitreykjavik.is
www.icelandguest.com/travel-guide/

More cool places I want to visit on our trip

1.
2.
3.
4.
5.
6.
7.
8.
9.
10.
11.
12.
13.
14.
15.

Who do I want to send postcards to?

Name:
Address:

Name:
Address:

Name:
Address:

Name:
Address:

Name:
Address:

Name:
Address:

Name:
Address:

Name:
Address:

Name:
Address:

Packing List

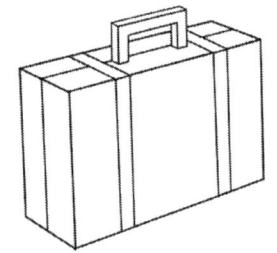

✓	This Book
	Tickets
	Passport
	Money
	Chargers
	Batteries
	Book to read
	Camera
	Tablet
	Sun glasses
	Sun cream
	Medication
	Jacket

	Toys
	Games
	Watch
	Snacks
	Umbrella
	Towel
	Guide book
	Add more below ...

Activities to do on the way to Iceland

Cool facts, word search and other fun activities

Answers and solutions are at the back of the book

Cool Facts About Iceland for Kids

- Iceland was founded by the Vikings. The Scandinavians were the first to settle in Iceland in 870

- Iceland became independent from the Kingdom of Denmark in 1918

- Iceland is covered by ice, glaciers and geysers and has more than 20 active volcanoes

- The largest volcano is called Vatnajokull which covers 8% of the country

- The ice of the glaciers is 1,000m thick

- Iceland has some farmland where you will see shee, they are the most common farm animals in Iceland

- You will also see a lot of seabirds like puffins. Puffins are black and white birds with large orange beaks that breed in large colonies on cliffs

- The population of Iceland is just over three hundred thousand people

- The capital city is Reykjavik, which means "smoky bay", it has 120,000 inhabitants

- The nickname of Iceland is "The Land of Fire and Ice"

- Hvannadalshnukur is the highest point in Iceland (2,119m)

- Hekla is Iceland's most active volcano; Hekla is also a common female name in Iceland

- The English word "geyser" comes from Iceland's Great Geysir in Haukadalur

- The phenomenon of the Northern Lights can be seen during mid-winter (November-December) when the weather is clear

- The last name of Icelanders is derived from their father's first name

- In the telephone book everyone is listed by their first name

Big Iceland Word Search

- Arnarstapi
- Gullfoss
- Latrabjarg
- Strandarkirkja
- Askja
- Jokulsarlon
- Leirhnjukur
- Blue Lagoon
- Lake Myvatn
- Perlan

G	P	B	C	V	H	V	M	S	V	B	J	Q	J	E	P
L	M	G	B	A	R	Z	S	C	L	L	J	S	O	P	X
C	E	K	R	C	S	O	Y	U	S	O	X	B	K	A	I
W	R	I	U	A	F	K	E	V	V	U	T	M	U	P	P
P	G	J	R	L	J	L	J	Z	L	X	Y	W	L	N	A
S	Q	S	L	H	A	B	G	A	A	O	M	Q	S	G	T
Y	N	U	G	G	N	T	A	V	Y	M	E	K	A	L	S
K	G	Z	O	E	A	J	B	R	F	D	R	R	R	P	R
I	F	O	Z	L	B	O	U	O	T	C	G	T	L	Y	A
F	N	P	E	R	L	A	N	K	C	A	B	X	O	A	N
U	P	Q	D	T	A	R	H	V	U	Q	L	U	N	N	R
W	N	C	P	R	G	T	P	Z	J	R	J	Y	U	T	A
C	I	Z	O	Y	G	B	Y	A	Q	K	T	J	R	K	N
S	T	R	A	N	D	A	R	K	I	R	K	J	A	V	B
E	V	J	G	H	R	M	Y	K	T	H	D	O	B	I	N
H	O	A	Y	T	I	R	R	Y	V	X	R	T	D	B	G

Great Iceland Crossword

Across

3. Common female name in Iceland

5. A waterfall located in the Hvita river

6. English word that comes from Iceland's Great Geysir

Down

1. Founders of Iceland

2. Most common farm animal in Iceland

4. Favorite sport in Iceland

Link Up Iceland

Link the letters, to make a word or phrase

Laki	Fox
Arctic	Lagoon
Northern	Zoo
Skogar	Myvatn
Reykjavik	Museum
Blue	Craters
Lake	Lights
The Golden	Farmhouse
Settlement	Circle
Hof	Center

Code Puzzle

Use the number codes to find names of cities and towns in Iceland (Tip 1=A, 2=B, 3=C)

18	5	25	11	10	1	22	9	11

1	11	21	18	5	25	18	9

11	5	6	12	1	22	9	11

7	18	9	14	4	1	22	9	11

1	11	18	1	14	5	19

19	5	12	6	15	19	19

Tile Puzzle

Rearrange the tiles to reveal the answer

Clue: Geothermal spa in Iceland

| UE | ON | BL | GO | LA |

Clue: A waterfall located in the South of Iceland

| LL | SS | GU | FO |

Clue: Largest volcano in Iceland

| JOK | NA | ULL | VAT |

Clue: They were the first to settle in Iceland

| VI | ANS | SCA | NA | NDI |

Mix Up

Unscramble each of the anagram clue words; each of them is a famous place in Iceland.

Copy the letters in the numbered cells to other cells with the same number to reveal the hidden message.

ULSARLONKOJ (Example)

J	O	K	U	L	S		R	L	O	N
					2					

SLFLUGOS

G	U		L	F		S	S
	11			7			

ERPNAL

P	E	R	L	A	
				4	

AJKRIKRADNARTS

S		R	A	N	D	A	R	K	I	R	K	J	A
	3												

24

RANRASTIPA

A	R	N		R	S	T	A	P	I
			5						

KIVAJKYER OOZ

R	E	Y		J	A		I	K	▓		O	O
			8			1						

LBUE GONOAL

B	L	E	▓		A	G	O	O	N
		9		10					

KSAAJ

A	S	K		A
			6	

Hidden Message

1	2	3	4	5	6	7	8	9	10	11

The Fallen Message Puzzle

Each letter appears in the correct column, but below where it should be.
You must put the letters back in the grid to rebuild the message.

		E		C		M			
	O		I		E		A		D
		E		J		Y			
	O		R		T		I	P	

				N		E	L			
	O	E	L	J	O	R	A			
T	O	U	I	C	T	M	I	N		
Y	W	E	R	C	O	Y	E	P	D	

26

Code Cracker

1. Solve the numbers puzzle

2. Convert the answer to a letter (1=A, 2=B, 3=C). Crack the secret code word.

				Number		Letter
4	+	3	=		=	
24	-	3	=		=	
9	+	3	=		=	
24	-	12	=		=	
5	+	1	=		=	
13	+	2	=		=	
29	-	10	=		=	
1	+	18	=		=	

Number Chains

1. Work out the math puzzle for each column below
2. Find the secret word, using the code (1=A, 2=B, 3=C)

35	3	17	22	11	7	15	8	20
-	+	+	-	-	+	+	-	+
25	12	4	11	3	23	3	4	5
=	=	=	=	=	=	=	=	=
+	-	+	-	+	-	-	+	-
23	2	6	5	1	20	16	18	6
=	=	=	=	=	=	=	=	=
-	-	-	+	-	+	+	-	-
24	10	22	6	8	4	2	17	1
=	=	=	=	=	=	=	=	=

Enter the letters above using the number code (1=A, 2=B, 3=C)

A-Mazing Maze

Can you find your way through the maze?

Color Iceland

Color the Flag

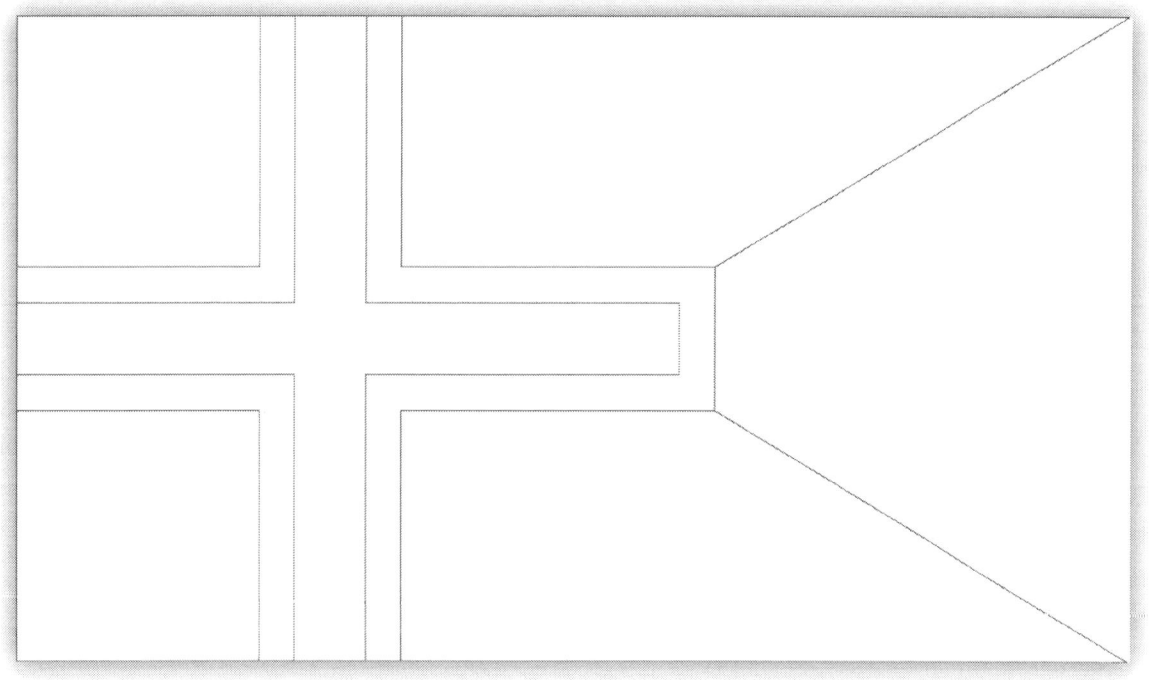

Colors: Red, White and Blue

Iceland Trip Diary
Write a daily diary during your trip

Day 1 Tip! Parents see page 83

Date: _____

Weather: _____

What we did today

_____

_____

_____

_____

_____

_____

Cool food of the day: _____

What I liked best today: _____

Funny thing of the day: _____

Draw something you saw today

My picture is of: _____

Day 2

Date: _____

Weather: _____

What we did today

_____
_____
_____
_____
_____
_____

Cool food of the day: _____

What I liked best today: _____

Funny thing of the day: _____

Draw something you saw today

My picture is of:

Day 3

Date: _____

Weather: _____

What we did today

_____

_____

_____

_____

_____

_____

Cool food of the day: _____

What I liked best today: _____

Funny thing of the day: _____

Draw something you saw today

My picture is of: _____

Day 4

Date: _____

Weather: _____

What we did today

_____
_____
_____
_____
_____
_____

Cool food of the day: _____

What I liked best today: _____

Funny thing of the day: _____

Draw something you saw today

My picture is of:

Day 5   Tip! Send your postcards

Date:

Weather:

What we did today

_____

_____

_____

_____

_____

_____

Cool food of the day:

What I liked best today:

Funny thing of the day:

Draw something you saw today

My picture is of: _____

Day 6

Date: _____

Weather: _____

What we did today

_____
_____
_____
_____
_____
_____
_____

Cool food of the day: _____

What I liked best today: _____

Funny thing of the day: _____

Draw something you saw today

My picture is of: _____

Day 7

Date: _____

Weather: _____

What we did today

_____

_____

_____

_____

_____

_____

_____

Cool food of the day: _____

What I liked best today: _____

Funny thing of the day: _____

Draw something you saw today

My picture is of: _____

Day 8

Date: _____

Weather: _____

What we did today

_____

_____

_____

_____

_____

_____

Cool food of the day: _____

What I liked best today: _____

Funny thing of the day: _____

Draw something you saw today

My picture is of: _____

Day 9

Date: _____

Weather: _____

What we did today

_____
_____
_____
_____
_____
_____
_____

Cool food of the day: _____

What I liked best today: _____

Funny thing of the day: _____

Draw something you saw today

My picture is of: _____

Day 10

Date: _____

Weather: _____

What we did today

_____

_____

_____

_____

_____

_____

_____

Cool food of the day: _____

What I liked best today: _____

Funny thing of the day: _____

Draw something you saw today

My picture is of: _____

Day 11

Date: _____

Weather: _____

What we did today

_____
_____
_____
_____
_____
_____
_____

Cool food of the day: _____

What I liked best today: _____

Funny thing of the day: _____

Draw something you saw today

My picture is of: _____

Day 12

Date: _____

Weather: _____

What we did today

_____

_____

_____

_____

_____

_____

_____

Cool food of the day: _____

What I liked best today: _____

Funny thing of the day: _____

Draw something you saw today

My picture is of: _____

Day 13

Date: _____

Weather: _____

What we did today

_____

_____

_____

_____

_____

_____

_____

Cool food of the day: _____

What I liked best today: _____

Funny thing of the day: _____

Draw something you saw today

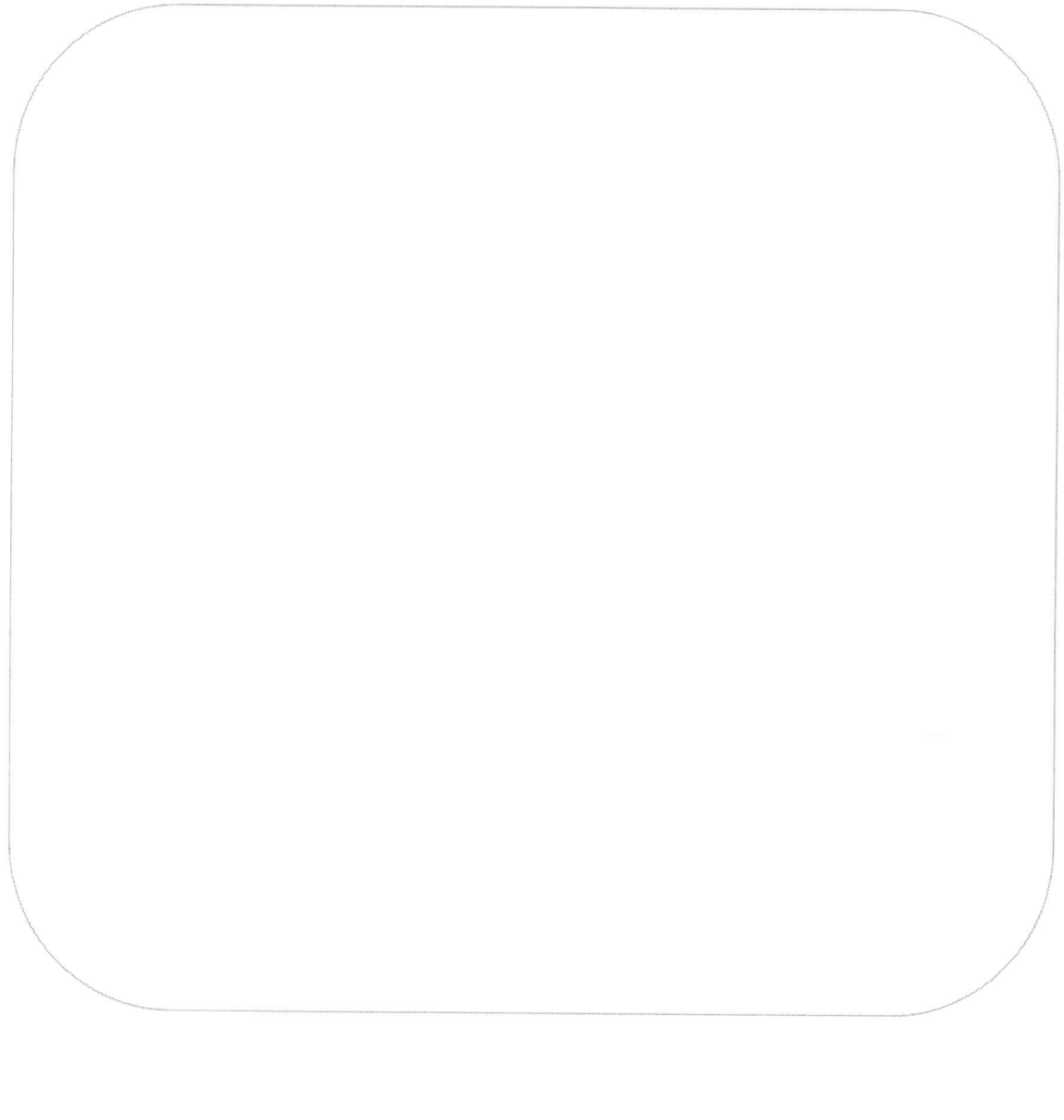

My picture is of: _____

Day 14

Date: _____

Weather: _____

What we did today

_____

_____

_____

_____

_____

_____

_____

Cool food of the day: _____

What I liked best today: _____

Funny thing of the day: _____

Draw something you saw today

My picture is of: _____

Activities for the Trip Home

Quiz, drawing and coloring fun, for your trip home

Answers and solutions are at the back of the book

Big Quiz

(Circle the correct answer)

1. The bright lights in the sky in Iceland during the winter months?

    Northern Lights   Western Lights

    Southern Lights   Eastern Lights

2. What is the only native mammal in Iceland?

    Dog   Cat

    Arctic fox   Cow

3. What is the favorite sport in Iceland?

    Volleyball   Soccer

    Basketball   Hockey

4. What is the common female name in Iceland?

    Maria   Hekla

    Isabel   Jasmin

5. Iceland's most active volcano

   Hekla   Katla

   Askja   Pinatubo

6. What is the capital city of Iceland?

   Reykjavik   Hekla

   Askja   Katla

7. Iceland's nickname

   Land of Paradise   Land of Fire and Ice

   Land of Gold   Land of the Goddess

8. What does Reykjavik means?

   Rainy bay   Slippery bay

   Smoky bay   Foggy bay

9. What is the approximate population of Iceland?

   500,000 people   700,000 people

   400,000 people   300,000 people

10. A black and white sea bird with large orange beak, found in Iceland

    Golden Plover   Arctic Tern

    Eagle   Puffin

11. Who were the first people to discover Iceland?

    Vikings   Chinese

    Americans   Japanese

12. Who were the first inhabitants to settle in Iceland?

    Spaniards   Mexicans

    Scandinavians   Americans

13. What is the official language of Iceland?

    Icelandic   French

    English   Japanese

14. What is the currency of Iceland

    Yen   Icelandic krona

    Peso   Dollar

Draw Iceland

Draw some of the cool things you saw in Iceland, during your trip

Color the Flag

Colors: Red, White and Blue

Things I will remember from our trip

Favorite Places we visited on our Trip

We hope you enjoyed your trip to Iceland

Don't forget to thank Mom and Dad

Useful Resources for Mom & Dad

Children's Shoe Sizes

UK	EUROPE	US	Japan
4	20	4½ or 5	12 ½
4 ½	21	5 or 5½	13
5	21 or 22	5½ or 6	13 ½
5 ½	22	6	13½ or 14
6	23	6½ or 7	14 or 14½
6 ½	23 or 24	7 ½	14½ or 15
7	24	7½ or 8	15
7 ½	25	8 or 9	15 ½
8	25 or 26	8½ or 9	16
8 ½	26	9½	16 ½
9	27	9½ or 10	16 ½ or 17
10	28	10½ or 11	17 ½
10½ or 11	29	11½ or 12	18
11 ½	30	12½	18 or 18 ½
12	31	13	19 or 19 ½
12 ½	31	13 or 13½	19 ½ or 20
13	32	1	20
13 ½	32 ½	1 ½	20 ½
1	33	1½ or 2	21
2	34	2½ or 3	22

Children's Clothing Sizes

UK	EUROPE	US	Australia
12m	80cm	12-18m	12m
18m	80-86cm	18-24m	18m
24m	86-92cm	23-24m	2
2-3	92-98cm	2T	3
3-4	98-104cm	4T	4
3-5	104-110cm	5	5
5-6	110-116cm	6	6
6-7	116-122cm	6X-7	7
7-8	122-128cm	7 to 8	8
8-9	128-134cm	9 to 10	9
9-10	134-140cm	10	10
10-11	140-146cm	11	11
11-12	146-152cm	14	12

Women's Shoe Sizes

UK	EUROPE	US	Japan
3	35 ½	5	22 ½
3 ½	36	5 ½	23
4	37	6	23
4 ½	37 ½	6 ½	23 ½
5	38	7	24
5 ½	39	7 ½	24
6	39 ½	8	24 ½
6 ½	40	8 ½	25
7	41	9 ½	25 ½
7 ½	41 ½	10	26
8	42	10 ½	26 ½

Women's Clothes Sizes

UK	US	Japan	France / Spain	Germany	Italy	Australia
6/8	6	7-9	36	34	40	8
10	8	9-11	38	36	42	10
12	10	11-13	40	38	44	12
14	12	13-15	42	39	46	14
16	14	15-17	44	40	48	16
18	16	17-19	46	42	50	18
20	18	19-21	48	44	52	20

Men's Shoe Sizes

UK	EUROPE	US	Japan
6	38 ½	6 ½	24 ½
6 ½	39	7	25
7	40	7 ½	25 ½
7 ½	41	8	26
8	42	8 ½	27 ½
8 ½	43	9	27 ½
9	43 ½	9 ½	28
9 ½	44	10	28 ½
10	44	10 ½	28 ½
10 ½	44 ½	11	29
11	45	12	29 ½

Men's Suit / Coat / Sweater Sizes

UK / US / Aus	EU / Japan	General
32	42	Small
34	44	Small
36	46	Small
38	48	Medium
40	50	Large
42	52	Large
44	54	Extra Large
46	56	Extra Large

Men's Pants / Trouser Sizes (Waist)

UK / US	Europe
32	81 cm
34	86 cm
36	91 cm
38	97 cm
40	102 cm
42	107 cm

Puzzles Answers and Solutions

Big Iceland Word Search

- Arnarstapi
- Gullfoss
- Latrabjarg
- Strandarkirkja
- Askja
- Jokulsarlon
- Leirhnjukur
- Blue Lagoon
- Lake Myvatn
- Perlan

G	P	B	C	V	H	V	M	S	V	B	J	Q	J	E	P
L	M	G	B	A	R	Z	S	C	L	L	J	S	O	P	X
C	E	K	R	C	S	O	Y	U	S	O	X	B	K	A	I
W	R	I	U	A	F	K	E	V	V	U	T	M	U	P	P
P	G	J	R	L	J	L	J	Z	L	X	Y	W	L	N	A
S	Q	S	L	H	A	B	G	A	A	O	M	Q	S	G	T
Y	N	U	G	G	N	T	A	V	Y	M	E	K	A	L	S
K	G	Z	O	E	A	J	B	R	F	D	R	R	R	P	R
I	F	O	Z	L	B	O	U	O	T	C	G	T	L	Y	A
F	N	P	E	R	L	A	N	K	C	A	B	X	O	A	N
U	P	Q	D	T	A	R	H	V	U	Q	L	U	N	N	R
W	N	C	P	R	G	T	P	Z	J	R	J	Y	U	T	A
C	I	Z	O	Y	G	B	Y	A	Q	K	T	J	R	K	N
S	T	R	A	N	D	A	R	K	I	R	K	J	A	V	B
E	V	J	G	H	R	M	Y	K	T	H	D	O	B	I	N
H	O	A	Y	T	I	R	R	Y	V	X	R	T	D	B	G

Great Iceland Crossword

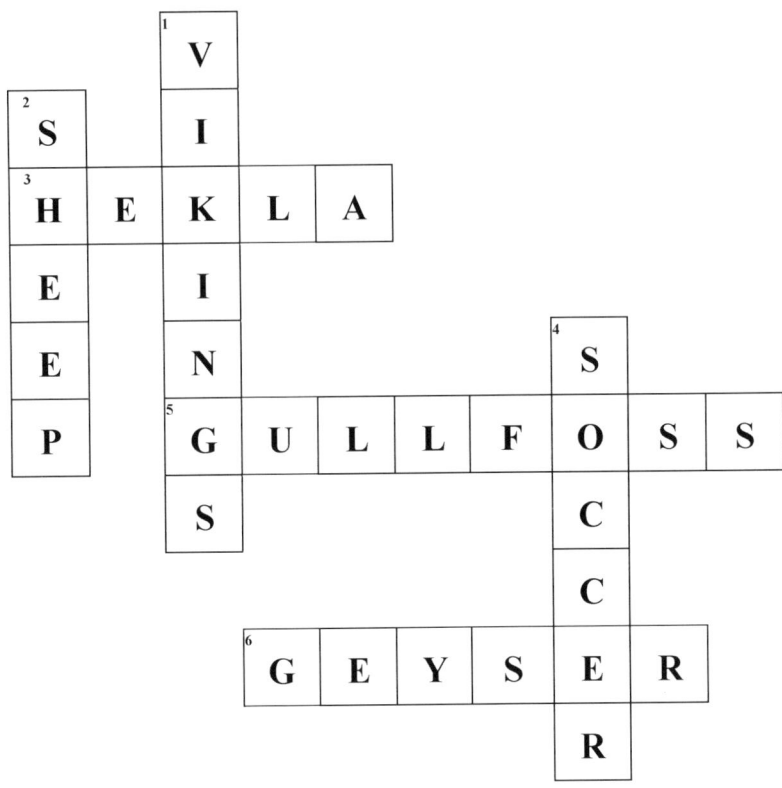

Across

3. Common female name in Iceland

5. A waterfall located in the Hvita river

6. English word that comes from Iceland's Great Geysir

Down

1. Founders of Iceland

2. Most common farm animal in Iceland

4. Favorite sport in Iceland

Link Up Iceland

Link the letters, to make a word or phrase

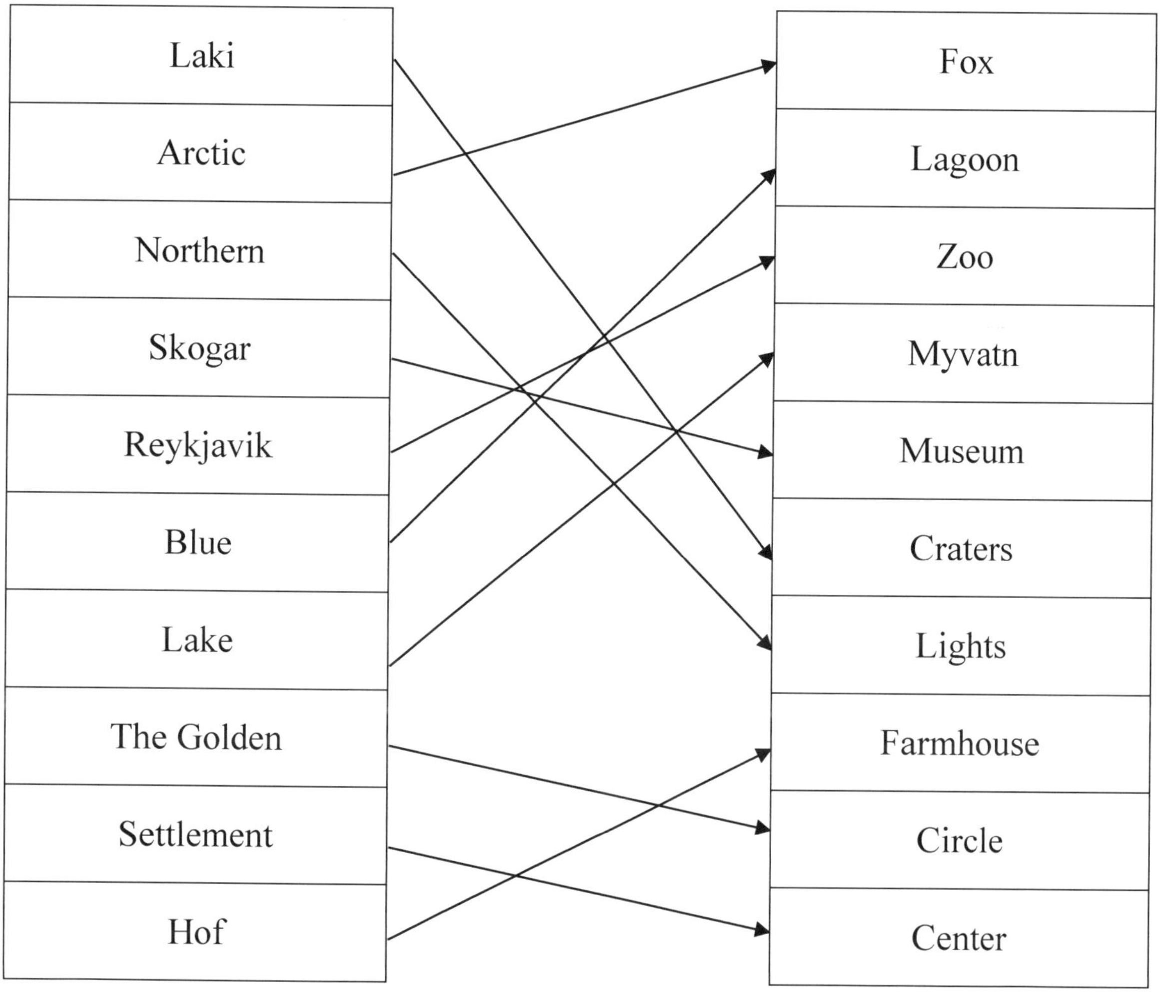

Laki	Fox
Arctic	Lagoon
Northern	Zoo
Skogar	Myvatn
Reykjavik	Museum
Blue	Craters
Lake	Lights
The Golden	Farmhouse
Settlement	Circle
Hof	Center

Code Puzzle

Use the number codes to find names of cities and towns in Iceland (Tip 1=A, 2=B, 3=C)

18	5	25	11	10	1	22	9	11
R	E	Y	K	J	A	V	I	K

1	11	21	18	5	25	18	9
A	K	U	R	E	Y	R	I

11	5	6	12	1	22	9	11
K	E	F	L	A	V	I	K

7	18	9	14	4	1	22	9	11
G	R	I	N	D	A	V	I	K

1	11	18	1	14	5	19
A	K	R	A	N	E	S

19	5	12	6	15	19	19
S	E	L	F	O	S	S

Tile Puzzle

Rearrange the tiles to reveal the answer

Clue: Geothermal spa in Iceland

| UE | ON | BL | GO | LA |

BLUE LAGOON

Clue: A waterfall located in the South of Iceland

| LL | SS | GU | FO |

GULLFOSS

Clue: Largest volcano in Iceland

| JOK | NA | ULL | VAT |

VATNAJOKULL

Clue: They were the first to settle in Iceland

| VI | ANS | SCA | NA | NDI |

SCANDINAVIANS

Mix Up

Unscramble each of the anagram clue words; each of them is a famous place in Iceland.

Copy the letters in the numbered cells to other cells with the same number to reveal the hidden message.

ULSARLONKOJ (Example)

J	O	K	U	L	S	A	R	L	O	N
					2					

SLFLUGOS

G	U	L	L	F	O	S	S
	11				7		

ERPNAL

P	E	R	L	A	N
				4	

AJKRIKRADNARTS

S	T	R	A	N	D	A	R	K	I	R	K	J	A
3													

RANRASTIPA

A	R	N	A	R	S	T	A	P	I
				5					

KIVAJKYER OOZ

R	E	Y	K	J	A	V	I	K	▓	Z	O	O
			8			1						

LBUE GONOAL

B	L	U	E	▓	L	A	G	O	O	N
		9		10						

KSAAJ

A	S	K	J	A
		6		

Hidden Message

V	A	T	N	A	J	O	K	U	L	L
1	2	3	4	5	6	7	8	9	10	11

The Fallen Message Puzzle

Each letter appears in the correct column, but below where it should be.
You must put the letters back in the grid to rebuild the message.

	W	E	L	C	O	M	E		
T	O		I	C	E	L	A	N	D
		E	N	J	O	Y			
Y	O	U	R		T	R	I	P	

				N		E	L			
	O	E	L	J	O	R	A			
T	O	U	I	C	T	M		I		N
Y	W	E	R	C	O	Y	E	P		D

Code Cracker

1. Solve the numbers puzzle

2. Convert the answer to a letter (1=A, 2=B, 3=C). Crack the secret code word.

				Number		Letter
4	+	3	=	7	=	G
24	-	3	=	21	=	U
9	+	3	=	12	=	L
24	-	12	=	12	=	L
5	+	1	=	6	=	F
13	+	2	=	15	=	O
29	-	10	=	19	=	S
1	+	18	=	19	=	S

Number Chains

1. Work out the math puzzle for each column below
2. Find the secret word, using the code (1=A, 2=B, 3=C)

35	3	17	22	11	7	15	8	20
-	+	+	-	-	+	+	-	+
25	12	4	11	3	23	3	4	5
=	=	=	=	=	=	=	=	=
10	15	21	11	8	30	18	4	25
+	-	+	-	+	-	-	+	-
23	2	6	5	1	20	16	18	6
=	=	=	=	=	=	=	=	=
33	13	27	6	9	10	2	22	19
-	-	-	+	-	+	+	-	-
24	10	22	6	8	4	2	17	1
=	=	=	=	=	=	=	=	=
9	3	5	12	1	14	4	5	18

| I | C | E | L | A | N | D | E | R |

Enter the letters above using the number code (1=A, 2=B, 3=C)

Big Quiz

(Circle the correct answer)

1. The bright lights in the sky in Iceland during the winter months?

    Northern Lights   Western Lights

    Southern Lights   Eastern Lights

2. What is the only native mammal in Iceland?

    Dog   Cat

    Arctic fox   Cow

3. What is the favorite sport in Iceland?

    Volleyball   **Soccer**

    Basketball   Hockey

4. What is the common female name in Iceland?

    Maria   **Hekla**

    Isabel   Jasmin

5. Iceland's most active volcano

   Hekla   Katla

   Askja   Pinatubo

6. What is the capital city of Iceland?

   Reykjavik   Hekla

   Askja   Katla

7. Iceland's nickname

   Land of Paradise   **Land of Fire and Ice**

   Land of Gold   Land of the Goddess

8. What does Reykjavik means?

   Rainy bay   Slippery bay

   Smoky bay   Foggy bay

9. What is the approximate population of Iceland?

   500,000 people   700,000 people

   400,000 people   **300,000 people**

10. A black and white sea bird with large orange beak, found in Iceland

    Golden Plover   Arctic Tern

    Eagle   **Puffin**

11. Who were the first people to discover Iceland?

    Vikings   Chinese

    Americans   Japanese

12. Who were the first inhabitants to settle in Iceland?

    Spaniards   Mexicans

    Scandinavians   Americans

13. What is the official language of Iceland?

    Icelandic   French

    English   Japanese

14. What is the currency of Iceland

    Yen   **Icelandic krona**

    Peso   Dollar

Made in the USA
Lexington, KY
08 November 2018